This
book belongs
to

_____
_____

a
small child's
Book of Cozy Poems

*To Edie Weinberg,
for the care she gives all books
—C.S.*

Acknowledgments

"Morning," "My Little Dog," "My Kitten," "Politeness," "My Teddy Bear," "The New Muffler," "Reading," "Sleeping Outdoors," "Bedtime," and "My Family" by Marchette Chute. From RHYMES ABOUT US by Marchette Chute. Published 1974 by E.P. Dutton. Copyright © 1974 by Marchette Chute. Reprinted by permission of Elizabeth Hauser. "April Rain Song" by Langston Hughes. From COLLECTED POEMS by Langston Hughes. Copyright © 1994 by the Estate of Langston Hughes. Reprinted by permission of Alfred A. Knopf, Inc."Home! You're Where It's Warm Inside" by Jack Prelutsky. From THE RANDOM HOUSE BOOK OF POETRY FOR CHILDREN by Jack Prelutsky. Copyright © 1983 by Jack Prelutsky. Reprinted by permission of Random House, Inc."Song of the Bunnies" by Margaret Wise Brown. From NIBBLE, NIBBLE by Margaret Wise Brown. Copyright © 1959 by William R. Scott, Inc. renewed 1987 by Roberta Brown Rauch. Used by permission of HarperCollins Publishers. "Stars" and "Day Is Done" from THE BABY'S BEDTIME BOOK by Kay Chorao (1984). Published by E.P. Dutton. "Grandpa Bear's Lullaby" by Jane Yolen. From DRAGON NIGHT AND OTHER LULLABIES by Jane Yolen. Copyright © 1980 by Jane Yolen. Reprinted by permission of Curtis Brown Ltd.

The editors wish to thank Rachel Seed
for her help with this book.

a
small child's
Book of
Cozy Poems

Illustrated by
Cyndy Szekeres

Cartwheel
·B·O·O·K·S· ®

SCHOLASTIC INC.
New York Toronto London Auckland Sydney

Copyright © 1999 by Cyndy Szekeres.
All rights reserved. Published by Scholastic Inc.
SCHOLASTIC, CARTWHEEL BOOKS and the CARTWHEEL BOOKS
logo are trademarks and/or registered trademarks of Scholastic Inc.

Library of Congress Cataloging-in-Publication Data
A small child's book of cozy poems / compiled and illustrated by Cyndy Szekeres.
  p.   cm.
  "Cartwheel books."
  Summary: A collection of short poems by such writers as Margaret Wise
  Brown, Langston Hughes, Jane Yolen, and Marchette Chute, all
  illustrated with rabbits, mice, cats, bears, and other animals.
  ISBN 0-590-38364-7
  1. Children's poetry, American. 2. Children's poetry, English.
  [1. American poetry—Collections. 2. English poetry—Collections.]
  I. Szekeres, Cyndy.
  PS586.3.S6   1999
  811.008'09282—DC21   98-20800
                                                                  CIP
                                                                  AC

12 11 10 9 8 7 6 5 4 3 2 1   9/9 0/0 01 02 03 04

Printed in Singapore   46
First printing, March 1999

·Contents·

Morning

How pleasant it is
To see the light
Come in the window
And push out the night.

How splendid it is
To hear someone say
There will be pancakes
For breakfast today.

— *Marchette Chute*

7

I'm Glad the Sky Is Painted Blue

I'm glad the sky is painted blue
    And the earth is painted green,
With such a lot of nice fresh air
    All sandwiched in between.

                        —Anonymous

April Rain Song

Let the rain kiss you.
Let the rain beat upon your head with
　silver liquid drops.
Let the rain sing you a lullaby.
The rain makes still pools on the sidewalk.
The rain makes running pools in the gutter.
The rain plays a little sleep-song
　on our roof at night.
And I love the rain.

　　—*Langston Hughes*

Home! You're Where It's Warm Inside

Home! You're a special place;
    You're where I wake and wash my face,
Brush my teeth and comb my hair,

    Change my socks and underwear,
Clean my ears and blow my nose,
    Try on all my parents' clothes.

Home! You're where it's warm inside,
   Where my tears are gently dried,
Where I'm comforted and fed,
   Where I'm forced to go to bed,

Where there's always love to spare;
   Home! I'm glad that you are there.

                              — *Jack Prelutsky*

Hurt No Living Thing

Hurt no living thing;
   Ladybug, nor butterfly,
Nor moth with dusty wing,
   Nor cricket chirping cheerily,
Nor grasshopper so light of leap,
   Nor dancing gnat, nor beetle fat,
Nor harmless worms that creep.

—*Christina G. Rossetti*

My Little Dog

My little dog is dear to me.
  He has no faults that I can see.

He is the finest dog I know.
  And I quite often tell him so.

—*Marchette Chute*

My Kitten

Kitten, my kitten,
 Soft and dear,
I am so glad
 That we are here
Sitting together,
 Just us two,
You loving me
 And me loving you.

— *Marchette Chute*

Song of the Bunnies

Bunnies zip
　And bunnies zoom
Bunnies sometimes sleep till noon

Zoom Zoom Zoom
　All through the afternoon
Zoom Zoom Zoom
　This is the song of the bunnies.

Bunnies jump
  And bunnies run
Bunnies also sit in the sun
  This is the song of the bunnies.

—*Margaret Wise Brown*

My Family

Part of my family is grown-up and tall.
Part of my family is little and small.
I'm in the middle and pleased with them all.

— *Marchette Chute*

Politeness

I met a squirrel the other day
   And spoke to him in a friendly way.
I couldn't pat him on the head
   But I gave him several nuts instead.
He took them from me one by one
   And waved his tail when he was done,
And he was happy, I could tell.

We both behaved extremely well.

— *Marchette Chute*

My Teddy Bear

A teddy bear is a faithful friend.
    You can pick him up at either end.
His fur is the color of breakfast toast,
    And he's always there when you need him most.

— Marchette Chute

The New Muffler

Muffled in my muffler,
    Striding through the snow,
I am much admired
    Everywhere I go.

— *Marchette Chute*

Song for a Little Mouse

I'm glad our house is a little house,
 Not too tall nor too wide.
I'm glad the hovering butterflies
 Feel free to come inside.

—Christopher Morley

Reading

A story is a special thing.
  The ones that I have read,
They do not stay inside the books.
  They stay inside my head.

—*Marchette Chute*

Stars

I'm glad the stars are over me
    And not beneath my feet,
Where we could trample on them
    Like cobbles on the street.
I think it is a happy thing
    That they are set so far;
It's best to have to look up high
    When you would see a star.

                     —*Anonymous*

Sleeping Outdoors

Under the dark is a star,
    Under the star is a tree,
Under the tree is a blanket,
    And under the blanket is me.

— *Marchette Chute*

Grandpa Bear's Lullaby

The night is long
   But fur is deep.
You will be warm
   In winter sleep.

The cave is dark
   But dreams are bright
And they will serve
   As winter light.
Sleep, my little cubs, sleep.

—*Jane Yolen*

30

Bedtime

I like the things that come at night—
  Being tickled; a pillow fight;
Hearing stories told in bed,
  Or perhaps a chapter read;
Drinks of water, two or three;
  And my puppy close to me.

—Marchette Chute

Day Is Done

Day is done,
   Gone the sun—
From the earth,
   From the hills,
From the sky.
   All is well,
Safely rest.
   God is nigh.

   —Anonymous